THE

MW01005605

WHITE GUY'S GUIDE TO EBONICS

BY
I. B. WHITE

CCC PUBLICATIONS

Published by
CCC Publications
9725 Lurline Avenue
Chatsworth, CA 91311

Manufactured in the United States of America

Cover ©1997 CCC Publications

Cover/Interior production by Oasis Graphics

ISBN: 0-57644-060-5

If your local U.S. bookstore is out of stock, copies of this
book may be obtained by mailing check or money order for
$5.95 per book (plus $2.75 to cover postage and handling)
to: CCC Publications; 9725 Lurline Avenue, Chatsworth,
CA 91311

Pre-publication Edition – 5/97

INTRODUCTION

O.K., I'm an old, fat white guy. But, I figured somebody would come up with this sooner or later, and better me than Saturday Night Live.

Having been brought up in Oakland, CA., and living there for 30+ years, I heard (and spoke) my share of what is now being referred to as *Ebonics.* We, as kids and teenagers, talked this way just because it was cool (or maybe it was just to bug our parents).

The funniest part, of course, was being "busted" for trying to be cool by Black friends who were just naturally cool. My constant misuse or mispronunciation of a hip word would send "those in the know" into fits of laughter. We used to sit around in multi-ethnic groups and try to "cap" on one another by seeing who could cut someone the lowest, either sexually or racially. I don't know, maybe it was a "guy" thing, or maybe it was just peculiar to the area of Oakland that I grew up in (close to Oakland High), but I suspect not. (I still don't know what "cap" means, but I assume its probably the same as "dis", but in a humorous manner–at least it always brought a laugh or an Oooo! in our crowd.) My thought is that this activity probably was a combination of a couple of things: discovery of our new-found sexuality, discovery that the folks who lived around us were not all exactly like ourselves, and, at least for me, the discovery that making people laugh made us feel good. In any case, it seems I never outgrew this sport.

While writing this I started thinking about the movie "White Men Can't Jump." In many ways, I think, it reflects the sort of environment I grew up in (especially the part about me not being able to get off the ground), and, I believe, the bittersweet experiences many of us old "city" fogies remember. We had a great time back then and I can't figure out what changed.

Maybe people are taking themselves too seriously. Maybe people are not appreciating, enjoying or laughing at their differences. Maybe people are hating these differences instead. I hope not.

I also hope people don't take this little book too seriously. I wrote it to make people of *all* ethnic backgrounds laugh (also for the money). As you can tell, some of the definitions are right on the mark, but many of them are from my own twisted little imagination.

Finally, it is my ultimate hope that readers do not lose sight of the main purpose of this book – which is simply to *have fun*.

A

abode: a board or a piece of lumber, as in "Hand me abode and some nails, Jim."

abrogate: the gate the bros use, as in, "That's abrogate—the sister use the other one."

affix: getting ready, as in "I'm affixin' to go to work."

Afro: 1.a throw. Also, 2. a hairstyle.

ah: I, as in," Ah'm cool."

albino: very, very, white, as in, "I ain't datin' no albino lookin' bitch!" See also: honky.

akkin: acting, as in "that girl akkin crazy!"

anenome: not a friend, as in, "That mean looking fella over there is anemone of mine."

apiece: a firearm, as in, "I'll be carrying apiece in case her boyfriend shows up."

arapaho: a rap singer of the female persuasion.

arn: an iron, as in, "I need you to arn me a shirt before I go out."

asbestos: a description of ones efforts, as in "He's doing asbestos he can."

ashore: I sure, as in "Ashore would like another helping of that pie."

aside: a rack of ribs.

asset: I sit, as in "Asset right in front of that other girl."

assure: a phrase meaning "I would," as in, "Assure'd love 50-yard line Rainder seats!"

asthma: as my, like: "Asthma friends are coming over, please try and act like an adult for a change."

attune: a song.

aw-ite: all right, as in, "How's that ho feeling today?" "She's aw-ite."

ax: ask, as in "Don't ax me no more questions."

B

back: buttocks, butt, backside. "That girl got back" means that the young lady has a real nice rear end.

backhoe: instructions on where to put something, as in, "Put my stuff in the backhoe, I don't want people messin' with it."

bad: good, as in "That girl is b-a-a-ad." This really means she is very good.

bag: 1. girlfriend, as in, "I got me a brand new bag." Also, 2. thing, as in a job or way of life, as in, "Engineering is my bag, mister."

basin: basing, as in,"Don't be basin your opinion on heresay."

battree: battery, as in, " My car has a dead battree."

B-ball: basketball.

befo': The year after a child turns three, then he befo'.

beeline: not telling the truth, as in, "Why you beeline to me, child? You know you hit your sister."

benign: The year after you be eight, then you benign.

bewitch: a question, as in, "You bewitch team?"

betroom: the place where one goes to sleep.

biddy: busy, as in, "Don't be listening to that ol' biddybody!"

bidnez: business, as in "I'm a bidnezman', or,"Why can't you take care of bidnez?"

birfday: birthday.

bitch: anyone of the female persuasion. Also, if used in reference to a male, an inference that one is gay. An even further insult would be "half-bitch", meaning half a man.

black hat: condom, as in, "You better be wearin' that black hat tonite hon, in case you meet up with some easy money."

blee': believe, as in "I blee' thats my seat, bro'."

bleed: a familiar term addressing one's friend, as in "Hey bleed, long time, no see."

blood: see also bleed, another term for a friend, as in, "Whuzzup, blood?"

blood pressure: what one basketball/football player might say if his teammate was not guarding his opponent very well, "Hey blood, pressure that guy!"

bloodshot: What might be said after a basketball player put up a good shot, "OOO, you see that bloodshot?"

blood sucker: this word is best left to one's own imagination.

blood test: any test taken by a friend, as in, "This blood test positive for the virus—he needs to be admitted!"

bloon: balloon.

bluegrass: someone smoked weed, as in, "He bluegrass."

bof': both, as in, "Bof' his his feet stink!"

bof'us: both of us, as in, "Bof'us are going shopping."

boo: marijuana, pot, grass, smoke, weed, dope, etc., as in, "Who got boo? You? That's coo'."

boo: an expression meaning, "Hello...is anybody home?",or, "I Know" as in, "Your finger's bleeding!" "Boo!"

boodle: one's (or someone else's) money, usually alot.

boody: body or butt, as in "Oooo, she got a nice boody." Also see booty.

booty: body, also sex, as in, "I'm gonna git me some booty tonite!"

bootang: when you are trying to "git you some," what you are try to get (See: git you some).

bootay: see boody, but extra nice.

boogabear: an ugly woman. A very ugly woman.

bra: brother, used as a term of equality, as in "Hey, bra, your woman is looking fine tonight!"

brad: wife, as in, "This is Melissa, my new brad."

braid: bread.

brang: bring, as in "Brang me that Thang."

bran': brand, as in "This great outfit is bran' new."

brefus': breakfast.

bress/bresses: breast/breasts. No further definition is given due to the touchiness of this/these subject/subjects.

brick: a terrible basketball shot, usually clanging off the backboard like a brick. It is generally acknowledged that bricks are only thrown up by white boys, but this is highly disputed in some circles.

bricklayer: one who throws up a lot of bricks.

brim: a hat, as in, "You think if I wear this new brim, I might be gettin' some trim?"

bro: see bra—this is the "original" term of endearment for one's close friend or brother, usually reserved for members of one's own ethnic group.

brochure: a secure brother, as in, "That brochure of hisself."

brotha/my brotha: brother/my brother, as in "That is one serious looking automobile, my brotha." See also: bro.

bump: to groove, to move with the music, as in, "That girl is sumpin – just look at her bumpin!"

buss: break, as in, "Don't buss your butt", or, "I'm gonna buss you you in the mouth."

C

cain't: cannot, as in "I cain't see the road its so dark."

chess: chest, as in, "That lady got one nice looking chess set!"

chestnut: one who is absolutely crazy about bresses.

chide: child, as in, "This my oldest chide, Clyde."

chidren: children, as in, "Now chidren, don't be be playing with your sister's chess set."

chill: a directive to be cool, as in, "Chill out, man, I'm sure the police only stopped us to ask for directions."

chillin: 1. relaxing, hanging out. 2. one's children.

chump: another word for a fool, a punk or someone who just isn't cool, as in, "Listen, chump, if you don't quit seeing my sister, I'll be on yo' ass!"

clout: cloud, as in, "That beautiful clout is shaped just like your booty!"

coat: court, as in, "I'll be seeing you in coat," or, "Let's go down to the coat and shoot some hoops."

cone: corn, as in "conebread."

coo: cool, hip, as in "Thats coo."

corner: the last few drops of liquor remaining in the bottom of a bottle. (Originally a square bottle, but now any bottle.)

Corner: the guy who works with dead boodies at the County Morgue.

cracker: a white boy, as in, "This player you brought ain't nothing but a cracker. Can he play?"

crew: the guys one hangs around with, the posse, the gang, as in, "Isn't my crew just a nice looking group of upstanding individuals?"

crib: one's house, as in, "Why don't we hang at your crib 'cause it's near all those hoochie-mamas?"

crouch: one's crotch, as in, "Man, my crouch aches just thinking about those hoochies!"

crutch: a device used for holding the small end of a marijuana cigarette.

D

da: the, as in "Could you you please shut da do'?" (door)

daid: dead, as in "His daddy's daid."

dank: smoke, marijuana, as in, "That be some rank dank man!"

dap: the current "gimme five," as in, "Dap me, bro'."

dat: that, as in "Don't do me like dat."

dawg: foot, as in, "My dawgs ache after a long hot day chasing bootay."

day: they, as in "Day ought to be coming any minute now."

daydream: several people dreaming, as in, "Daydream of owning a large boat in the islands."

28

debark: 1. what de dogs do. 2. What is on de tree trunk.

debate: what you put on de hook when you fish.

decrease: what you want when you iron your pants.

deduce: the playing card in the deck right after de ace.

def': cool, as in, "That Jeff is def'." Now if Jeff is hearing impaired, however, you may want to just say he's cool.

deface: if you're mad at someone this is what you get into.

default: if it's not your fault then it's default of someone else.

defeat: what one puts their socks and shoes on.

defer: politically incorrect, but a coat made from animal skins.

defile: 1. what one uses to trim fingernails or to remove material from wood or metal. 2. also, a place to put record documents such as tax forms.

defrosting: the sweet confectionary spread usually put on a cake.

defuse: 1.the circuit interrupter in an electrical system, 2. what you would light if you had a firecracker or bomb.

degrade: 1. what one usually receives if one completes one's classes. 2. the classification or rating of an item such as meat or steel, etc., as in, "What is degrade of this hamburger?"

deice: the jewels.

delay: 1. how the geography of the earth looks, such as delay of de land. 2. derogatory word for one's bedmate or companion.

delight: the light, as in,"Turn off delight, got dammit."

dems: them, as in, "Are you sure dems my shoes under the bed?"

demean: a desription of someone not nice, such as "demean old man."

demote: the water surrounding the castle, as in, "Watch out for demote 'cause I am not a great swimmer!"

denial: the river that carried the boat where Cleopatra and Mark Antony were "gittin' some."

denote: a short written document, as in, "Denote reads, 'I think you have a nice bootay'."

depart: one's role in a movie, such as, "I got depart."

deport: 1. where one usually boards de boat. Also, 2. a sweet wine, as in, "Man, did I drank all deport?"

deride: mode of transportation, usually one's automobile.

descent: the smell, as in, "I love descent you're wearing."

despise: agents from another country who are after your secrets.

detail: the rear end of anything, such as an animal or airplane. "I'd like a seat near detail please."

detest: after studying for a class, you are usually given detest—a certifcation of your knowledge.

detour: when one is visiting unknown areas and wishes to learn more about a certain place, one would ask for detour. This is usually given by detour guide.

device: second in command, such as device president or device principal.

devote: the ballot one would cast toward a candidate in a democatic type of election.

di (pronounced dee): the, as in, "Di rain in Spain falls mostly on di plain."

Ditneyland: Disneyland.

dig: to understand or figure it out, as in, "Nowumsayn, bro,?" "I dig."

dis: 1. this, as in, "Dis is mine, not yours." 2. to disrespect or insult someone, as in, "Don't dis me bro'."

disarm: describing ones appendage, such as "Disarm hurts, not the other one."

disband: a reference to a musical group, such as, "Disband is coo'!"

disbar: a reference to a drinking establishment, such as, "Disbar has the best margaritas!"

discredit: a reference to ones credit, such as, "Discredit card is over its damn limit!"

disdain: a reference to a spill or mark that has left a permanent discoloration: "Disdain is grape juice – it ain't never gonna come out!"

disfavor: a kindness shown to someone, as in, "Could you do me disfavor?"

dishevel: a tool used for digging holes or clearing sidewalks, as in, "Dishevel sure be heavy."

disjoint: a reference to a marijuana cigarette– "Disjoint ain't lit—could you light it for me bro'?"

dismember: 1. a reference to one who belongs to a group or a club. 2. a reference to ones own (male) genitalia.

dismiss: a reference to a proper young lady, such as, "Dismiss would like another drink of water please."

dismount: What a cowboy might call his date, especially if she were rather large.

disorder: 1. a request for food or drink at a restauant or bar, as in, "disorder must be wrong—I don't even like Olde English 800." 2. a command by a superior if one is in any of the armed services, as in, "Disorder must be obeyed or yo' ass is mine!"

displace: wherever you are (as opposed to dat place). For example, "Displace serves the best ribs in town."

disrobe: a reference to a nightime coverup, as in, "disrobe you bought me barely covers my bresses."

dissent: the aroma, as in, " I smelled dissent before and it's worse than a 3 day old pair of unnapants!"

disservice: 1. reference to the act of serving; "Disservice sucks in this restaurant."

disuede: talking about the material in a piece of leather clothing; "disuede in this jacket is sooo soft."

distaste; a reference to the flavor of something, as in, "Distaste awful!"

distinct: a reference to an event that did not turn out well: "How did you like your dinner sir?" …. "Distinct!"

divisible: all those items that are discernable to the naked eye.

division: 1. what one has when one is able to use one's eyes. 2. a dream or hope of the future.

do': door, as in "Could you ho' di do'?"

do: (pronounced dew): hairdo/haircut, as in "Your new 'do look like it caught on fire and someone tried to put it out with a hatchet."

dog: to annoy, bug or follow someone, as in "Don't dog me, man, or I'll bust your chops!"

Don Ho: Don's girlfriend, as in, that's Don Ho he's with."

dope: cool, as in, "That weed is dope!" Not usually a good idea to call something dope in front of the police, however.

'do-rag: a scarf worn over one's 'do to keep it from getting dirty /windblown etc. Sometimes worn by any youthful male trying to be coo'.

doubloon(s): reference to the balloon(s), as in, "Doubloons she bought look an awful lot like condoms, don't you think?"

downtown: in basketball, to take someone all the way down the court, embarass them with one's moves, and then score spectacularly on them.

doze: those, as in, "Doze cupcakes are not for you."

drank: drink, as in, "I sure could use a drank."

draws: underwear, as in "Why don't you wash your draws, bro'?"

drug: pulled, as in, "He done drug that suitcase all the way from the airport."

dunk: in basketball, to jam the ball down thru the hoop by jumping above the rim. Not usually attainable by white boys unless over about 6′3.″ See also slam, jam, phi slamma jamma.

E

ease: move, as in, "Why
don't you ease you bad self
on over here next to me?"

easy money: an easy score,
in any number of ways:
"She's easy money," or,
"That shot's easy money."

equipment: another of the many ways men of all color reference their genitalia. Usually, they in some way emphasize how extraordinary it is, such as, " Oh, you got to check out my heavy equipment, sweetlips."

F

fax: facts, as in, "Those are really the fax, officer."

face: face, used to describe when someone is confronting you, such as, "I'll be in your face, man."

factry: the place where manufacturing takes place, as in, " My girlfriend makes jimmies in the rubber factry."

feen: someone who is really into drugs or sex (drug feen, sex feen).

ferreal: honest or sincere, as in, "That brother is ferreal." See also: freel.

fiddy: fifty, as in, "Gimme fiddy dollars for the grocery store."

fitty: fifty, as in, "My wife looks like fitty 'cause she got skinny legs, but she's only twenny."

fit: fifth, as in, "This is the fit time I asked you to be quiet!"

flo': floor, as in, "Get up off the flo' before I tan your hide!"

flow: floor, as in, "He flew thru the do' and flat on the flow!" See also: flo'.

flouride: Florence's car.

fo': four, as in, "I'll throw in fo' tires with that car."

foe: for, as in, "What did you do that foe, bro'?"

foin: fine, as in, "That mama sure is lookin' foin!"

fonky: not right, not good, as in, "Don't be giving me no fonky weed, man."

foreclose: a clothing allowance, as in, "I gave you twenny bucks foreclose and you spent it already?"

fortify: what comes after forty-four, as in, "I just gave you fortify foreclose."

fraud: fried, as in, "Why don't you cook us up a mess of fraud eggs, dear?"

freak: to party, to dance or to make love: "Do you wanna freak wit' me?"

free: the number that falls between two and four.

freel: a question, asking if someone is sincere or if something is really true: "My dog died when he ate my horny toad." "Freel?"

fonky: not good, as in "That ol' dress is fonky!"

funky: fonky, but not used anymore, except by aging hippies.

fuss: first, as in, "Don't be cuttin' in line, I was here fuss!"

fussin': 1. making a big deal out of something, such as "Quit fussin' about the fact that I shot your dog." 2. getting in one's face, such as "Don't be fussin' at me 'cause I shot your dog."

G

G: home boy, someone from your neighborhood that you associate with, as in, "Say G, whuzzup witchu? Any bootay in the hood?"

git: get, as in, "Git your butt on home before I whup you!"

gittin' you some: an indication that you will be having sex, as in, "Now son, will you be gittin' you some this evening?"

goot: good, as in "This is certainly a goot bowl of soup."

gots: has/have, as in,"I gots to get to the office as I have an urgent appointment with my attorney."

granite: granted, as in, "My first husband took me for granite."

grey poupon: gittin' you some, as in, "How about a little grey poupon, Miss?"

groove on: actually "gittin' some."

gubmint: government, as in, "As far as I'm concerned, the gubmint is really just a swell bunch of guys."

gwan: going/gone, as in, "Don't ask me where William gwan."

H

haid: head, as in, "That man certainly has an odd shaped haid."

hail: hell, as in, "Working at this place has been pure hail."

half-bitch: an insult, to infer that a man is half woman, as in, "Stop actin' like a half-bitch and get over here so I can whup on you!"

hamma: hammer, a tool used for hitting, as in, "I"m gonna hamma that man if he comes home drunk agin!"

Heidi Ho: conceal the woman, as in, "Heidi Ho before her husband comes looking for her."

hep: help, as in, "I think I'll hep myself to some more of this yummy paté."

herb: marijuana, pot, weed, smoke, hemp, etc., as in, "I could use some righteous herb before I meet that old skeezer!"

hisself: a reference to one's self, as in "He was able to put on his pants by hisself."

homeboy: a friend or associate from one's neighborhood.

homey: a homeboy, one from the neighborhood, as in, "You want him to do WHAT? You know homey don't play that!"

homo: an instruction to one's girlfriend or wife to cut the lawn.

hoochie-mama: a slut, or dressed like one anyway.

hoop/hoops: basketball, as in "Lets play some hoop," or, "Lets shoot a few hoops."

hose: a group of several women, as in "Lets go check out them hose."

hotel: a reference to a woman to say something, as in, "Hotel that man I'm your husband."

huzbin: husband, as in, "Hotel that man I'm your huzbin."

68

I

Idaho: 1.one of the states. 2. a sure way to start an argument: " Watchyoumean, Idaho? You da ho, and furthermore your momma's a ho!"

igorant: ignorant, stupid, as in, "I'm not as igorant as you look!"

impotent: important, as in, " I got impotent work to do."

income: a description of one's entrance, as in, "I was just kissing my girlfriend when income my wife."

inyoface: an exclamation, usually stated after you have jammed a basketball over someone or "gotten on" someone after they have done something you feel is wrong.

iota: I should.

isolate: a statement made when one is not on time.

Ivanhoe: Ivan's girlfriend.

J

jack: 1. a familiar term for one's peer. 2. a familiar term for one's enemy. 3. when used as a verb, a term for beating someone up, as in, "I'm gonna jack you up!"

jam: 1. to dunk or stuff a basketball (see dunk), as in, "I'm gonna jam this sucker from half court right after I jump over you, your momma, and your Uncle Jojo!"

jest: just, as in, "That's jest the way it is, my brother."

jimmy: condom, as in, "Jump into a jimmy, Jimmy, before you get that bootang."

jive: not real, not sincere communication, as in, "Don't jive me about getting married, sucker, or I'll cut you up like a Benihana entree!"

jint: (rhymes with pint) joint, or marijuana cigarette, as in, "I'd love to smoke a jint witchu before we get some sweet stuff."

jonk: junk, as in, "This car you sold me is a piece of jonk!"

joker: someone not to be taken seriously: "Do you blee' this joker thinks he can jam it over me?"

jubilee: another way of saying "Do you believe?": "Jubilee this weather we been having?"

juicy: another way of saying "Do you see?": "Juicy the bootay on that girl?"

july: a query as to whether one is telling the truth: "July about my girlfriend?"

K

keel: kill, as in, "You touch my old lady and I'll keel you and and all your relatives!"

kilt: killed, as in, "That dog just kilt my favorite cat!"

kine: kind, as in, "Stay away from her, she's just not kine."

L

lack: like, as in "My, it looks lack serious rain today."

lame: stupid/not cool, as in, "That joke is as lame as your old three-legged dawg."

Laud: Lord, as in, "Goot Laud, that man got a lot of money!"

lef: 1. left, as in, "My baby up and lef me, just like that." 2. left, as in, "I throw with my lef hand."

les: let us, as in, "Les jump into our jimmies, Jimmy, before we look for some easy money, honey."

lesson: unless: "Lesson we practice on the computer, we won't be able to pass this class."

libel: liable, as in, "We're libel to miss the town unless you stop and ask for directions, dear."

links: most any type of sausage. 2. belonging to the tall member of the "Mod Squad."

Load: Lord, as in, "Goot Load, that girl got some bootay!"

lilac: combination of a verb and adjective to describe ones truthfulness: "You lilac a dog. You lilac a rug. You just a plain lie."

lout: loud, as in, "Would you mind not playing your music so lout?"

M

mah: my, as in, "Get your stinking hands offa mah booty!"

main man: 1. one's best friend, as in, "This here's my main man because he got me a fine position with an Accountancy Firm."

malign: 1. possessive for the string one uses for fishing. 2. one's part in a play, such as, "When do I say malign?"

maroon: possessive for one's personal place in one's house: "I'm going to maroon to sleep."

mat: might, as in, "I mat go run to the store", or, "Those are some matty fine sisters standing over there."

melodious: a statement about the way Mel smells. (Mel stinks).

mo: more, can be used in any combination of items– mo money, mo cars, mo lester, etc.

moaning: a greeting to another performed before noon.

mohair: a comparison of the amount of head coverage one has: "Larry has mohair than you."

morass: a comparison of the amount of rear end that one has: " "Sheila has morass than you."

mos': most, as in, "I know mos' of my algebra homework." Also: mosly, as in "I'm mosly just relaxing."

motivate: move, as in, "Why don't you motivate your ass on outta here before I kick it?"

mtpp: short for "gittin you some" (mashing the poon-poon)

muss: must, as in, " I simply muss try a piece of that scrumptious looking smoked salmon."

my bad: my mistake, as in, "That was your face I just jammed the basketball into? Oops, my bad!"

N

nane: name, as in, "What's your nane, young lady?"

natcho: not yours, as in, "Thats natcho cheese, it's mine."

natcherly: naturally, as in "I have natcherly trusted you to handle this matter."

net: a word in basketball used to describe when the ball goes through the hoop without touching it, hitting "nothing but net."

node: knew, as in, "I was almost sure I node him."

nondescript: not in the script, not part of the plan.

nowumsayn: do you understand me?, as in, "You are dating one ugly woman, nowumsayn?"

nuttin: either a response to a question as to "What are you doing?" or, when added to the word "honey," a sweetened breakfast cereal.

O

obscene: I've seen, as in,"obscene this movie before."

obstruct: I've struck, as in, "Goot Lawd, I think obstruct gold!"

ode: when one man has borrowed money from another: "I ode him twenny dollars."

off: to kill, as in "I hope they don't decide to off me because I ode him twenny dollars!"

offen: off, as in, "Get offen me, you big, fat lout!"

ole: old, as in "This ole piece of crap ain't gonna get us to the corner, let alone Didneyland!"

ottoman: one should, as in, "Should we go out for a few cocktails?" "We ottoman because I'm pretty sure there are a couple of boogabears waitin' for us at home tonight."

P

pacific: specific, as in, "You got to be more pacific."

pah: pie, as in, "I sure could eat a big old slice of apple pah."

pasteurize: when someone asks you how deep you're in it, and you know it's over your head, you answer "pasteurize."

penis: the instructions a doctor gives one when he hands one a specimen cup.

pick: 1. a comb with long teeth. 2. in basketball, blocking the path of an opponent, also known as a "screen." 3. a "pick n' roll" is when you finish combing your hair and then head out in your car for some action.

pisstivity: state of angriness. When you are extremely angry, you are known to be in "a high state of pisstivity."

pig: a highly regarded member of a law enforcement agency.

ponk: a punk, or someone you don't like and would prefer to beat up, as in, "Don't mess with me, ponk, or I'll jack you up!"

program: what one should be doing in order to fit in, as in "Get with the program, fool!"

protein: any organized professional group of athletes.

psych: 1. to fake one out. 2. to intmidate one, as in "Psych! You thought I was gonna kill you, but I'm only gonna maim you!"

Q

'q', 'que: barbeque, as in, "I'm going to the 'q' with this boogabear to see how much she can really eat."

R

rap: a style of music, as in, "You play that rap any louder and I'm gonna come up there and rap you on your head!"

rapper: the packaging around a candy bar.

reckless: without a means of transportation.

red: ready, as in,"Aren't you red to go to the movies yet?"

reefer: a marijuana cigarette, as in, "If I smoke that reefer, I'll empty your reefer."

retard: 1. to put new rubber on your vehicle, as in, " I just retard my Mercedes as the tars were lookin' kinda bald." 2. too old to work.

reverent: a minister, as in, " We just heard a sermon from Reverent Smith."

rhythm: what most white folks don't have.

row: corn row, a way of combing one's hair so the resultant style looks like mini rows of corn, as in, "That girl has a cute row, but she gotta have back to be fine."

S

samich: sandwich, as in, "I could really eat a big old fatty pork samich right now."

sags: pants, you know, the kind that miraculously stay up even though the belt line is far below the curve of the butt. How do they do that, anyway?

saline: an instruction to move or list to one side— "Saline on over here and check this out."

sane: same, as in, "Hey you got the sane last name as me."

sang: sing, as in, "And now we're going to sang Christmas carols."

sank: sink, as in, "Oh my, I'm so darn heavy I hope I don't sank in this pool."

satiate: a statement (or question) that a female has already eaten, as in, "You satiate? Man, it looks like she never stopped!"

seal: sill, as in, "I just hope she doesn't sit her big butt on that window seal."

seben: seven, as in, "I just need to run down to the seben-leben for a six-pack of malt liquor."

sebendy: seventy.

sec: a statement meaning "wait," or, "I'll be with you in a minute."

seed: the past tense of the verb see, to have visualized, as in, "I know you seed my girlfriend, because I can smell her perfume."

sef: self, as in, "I helped my sef to some more potatoes."

seldom: to exchange for money, as in, "I had a new pair of boots but I seldom."

sheit: an expletive, usually expressed in a long, drawn-out manner, such as: "Sh-eeee-it, that's one fine looking Excaliber!"

shif: shift, as in, "I hope he don't shif his weight, 'cause if he does this boat is going under!"

shifless: no good or worthless. Or, I suppose, it could mean an automatic transmission.

shit: one's stuff or belongings, as in, "Could you go get my shit out of the bedroom?" Amazingly, when one asks one's bro' to get " the shit", he knows exactly what the stuff is and brings it out.

sho': sure, as in, "You sho' you wouldn't like another helping of Yorkshire pudding?"

shore: sure, as in, "Yes, I'm shore."

side: 1. a rack of ribs, usually pork. 2. an ancient expression for a music album.(an album is ancient, too)

sista: a woman, especially a woman that you are fond of and to whom you can relate.

skeezers: unattractive women, as in, "I'll bet those skeezers got diseasers! I'll pass on a date!"

skin: a word used as part of an expression to greet someone, as in, "slip me some skin, bro'."

skonk: skunk, often used in conjunction with the words "shifless" and "no good" to point out that one is worthless.

slam: another word for "jam," or dunking a basketball, as in, "I'm gonna slam that ball so hard your teet' will rattle."

slate: an expression that it's not early.

sleeve: an expression that it's time for us to go.

slow: an expession that something is not high

smack: trash-talking, as in, "Don't be talkin' smack or I'll pop you!"

smelt: past tense of smell, as in, "That perfume smelt good."

smoke: 1. marijuana. 2. to kill, as in, "Lets smoke this punk."

snuff: a statement that a quantity of something is sufficient.

solit: (pronounced solitt) an expression that someting is fine, or in good shape, as in, "That woman is solit!"

soul brother: your only male sibling, as in," I have no sisters and this my soul brother."

splain: explain, as in,"You got some splainin' to do."

splay: an expression meaning "let's start the game."

sprung: excited, in the male (sexual) sense.

squat: nothing, as in, "Look, you don't know squat about nuthin'."

squeeze: one's companion—the favorite one being the main squeeze, as in, "This man is my main squeeze, but I got plenty of squeezins on the side."

stain: not goin'.

stank: to stink/smell, as in, "Oooo, your feet stank!"

stankho: an unattractive woman, as in "Ooooweee, she a stankho!"

sto': store, as in," Could you run to the sto' for me?"

stone: pretty, as in, "She is a stone fox."

stylin': looking good, as in, "With these orange plaid shorts and green striped shirt you know I'm stylin'."

sucka: sucker, as in, "I'm gonna whup you, sucka!"

sugar: some sweet love, such as a kiss–"How about a little sugar, Sugar?"

summo': some more, as in, Please give me summo french fries."

sumpin': something, as in, "Sumpin' fell on my head as I walked past the tree."

'sup: an expression meaning "What's happening?" or "How are you?", as in, "'Sup, sista? Lookin' goot!"

sweet: good, as in, "Oooo, that girl got a sweet booty."

T

tag: to spray paint, or to mark ones territory, as in, "Let's tag their 'hood with with a large, pink teddie bear so they know we're bad!"

taint: isn't.

tandem: spank them, as in, "If you don't get to bed right now, I'm going to tandem hides."

tang: woman/women, as in, "Thats some fine looking tang you're hanging with, my brotha."

tard: tired, as in, "After a long day of shopping my dogs are tard."

taste: just a little bit, as in, "Give me a taste of boodie and I'll be singing for daaays!"

tasty: good, as in, "Oooo, that was one tasty lookin' mamma."

teet: teeth, as in, "I guess I'll go on upstairs and brush my teet."

thang: 1. thing. 2. an expression that it's not a worry—"It's no thang."

theorize: Theo gets up.

therefore: there's four of them.

tine: time, as in, "It's tine to get up for school."

tis: (pronounced tiz) is, as in, "Your equipment is not very big!" "Tis so!" "Tis not!"

tole: told, as in, "I tole 'em tine and tine again to get to bed."

toot: tooth, as in, "If you don't leave me alone, I'm gonna knock out your toot!"

toss-up: a sexually active woman, as in, "I'm looking for a toss-up this evening because I really need a good shot of bootay!"

tree: the number that comes right after two and just befo' fo'.

trim: sex, as in, "I sure could use a little trim." "But you just got a haircut." "That's not what I mean, Dear."

twenny: twenty, as in, "You want twenny bucks for that smoke? No way, man."

U

udder: other, as in, "My key is in my udder pants."

unna: under, as in, "My key is unna my pants."

unnapants: underwear, as in, "My key fell outta my pants and into my unnapants."

unnapaid: underpaid, as in, "That fine ho is grossly unnapaid."

unnashirt: undershirt, as in, "This unnashirt is only three days old, dear, and I think it's good for another two anyway."

unnatow: undertow, as in, "Watch the unnatow, ho, or you gonna go."

unnawear: underwear, as in, "This unnawear too tight for my booty."

unsprung: not hard (see sprung).

upside: to hit alongside, as in, "Don't make me come over there upside your haid!"

uptight: tense or nervous, as in, "I'm feeling very uptight in my unnawear."

W

waffle: the wife will, as in, "The waffle take care of my jonk."

wassail: a question inquiring why one would want to use a boat.

wat: white, as in, "Ooo, that wat boy can jump!"

whateva': so what or who cares, as in,"You have the ugliest dog I have ever seen!" "Whateva'."

whup: whip, beat up, as in, "That boy so ugly he looks like he was whupped with the ugly forest!" (not the ugly stick or even the ugly tree...the whole forest)

whuzzat: what's that?

wit: with, as in, "I'm going wit her to the liquor store."

witchew: with you, as in, "What's up witchew, bro'?"

womens: woman, as in, "Don't be lookin' at my womens!"

wuzup: what's up, as in, "Wuzup with you, bro'?"

wuzzat: what's that, as in, "Wuzzat your sister I saw you with last night?"

X

X-Ray: 1. what Ray will be if he gets caught with Big George's wife. 2. a question directed at Ray, as in, "Please Big George, don't X-Ray where he's been."

Y

yo: your, as in, "Yo momma!"

yo ho: your girlfriend.

yorn: yours, as in " These ain't mine, they're yorn."

yos: to smoke, as in "I'm sorry, sir, but you'll have to put out that joint—this is a no yosing section."

youalie: a statement meaning you are not telling the truth, as in, "I didn't know she was yo ho." "Youalie!"

Z

zackly: exactly, as in, "That skeezer's not zackly what I had in mind when I said I needed bootay!"